MY FUTURES PAST

A SELF-GUIDED JOURNAL

My Futures Past: A Self-Guided Journal

Text © 2021 by Rachel Menefee

Oaso
Portland, Oregon

ISBN: 979-8-9853691-0-6
Library of Congress Control Number: 2021924372

Art © 2021 by Begoña Fernández Corbalán
begofernandezcorbalan.myportfolio.com

Editing and Design provided by Indigo: Editing, Design, and More
Proofreader: Ali Shaw
Cover and interior designer: Jenny Kimura
www.indigoediting.com

MY FUTURES PAST

A SELF-GUIDED JOURNAL

RACHEL MENEFEE

ILLUSTRATED BY BEGOÑA FERNÁNDEZ CORBALÁN

I HAVE STRUGGLED WITH MENTAL ILLNESSES IN MY LIFE THAT FORCED ME TO lose out on the idea of living. I wanted to be comfortable and unencumbered by my own limitations. So, I began writing about my childhood in great detail and was able to unravel memories that had shattered my inner child. I was able to identify PTSD that I was previously unaware of and finally understand why certain circumstances triggered me. I realized I'd developed unhealthy coping mechanisms and habits as a result of these traumatic life events. Finally, I noticed that I was projecting my fragmented self onto others in relationships that explicitly challenged the parts of myself that weren't healed.

Why am I telling you this? Because when writing in this journal, it's critical that you be completely honest with yourself. The part that you are shutting out is what most needs to be healed through writing.

AN UNFILTERED YOU

There are many guided journals that have questions that you must directly answer on each page. These questions, though useful, do not encourage you the writer to let your mind wander. They were derived from a narrative that was not your own.

This journal is a dedicated space where you can freely share your story and reflect on your experiences—all of the good, bad, and everything in between. At the end of the day, we know when we're ready to begin our healing process. I hope this journal can help you start that journey.

You deserve happiness. You deserve to be free from what has held you back.

BEFORE YOU BEGIN

By beginning this journal, you've shown graciousness toward yourself. It's an excellent first step toward self-healing. Recovering from years of trauma takes time, and the same is true for writing your story. Patience is a virtue since you already possess everything you require.

Consider yourself a gardener, and the plant being tended to throughout this book is your wound. You can allow yourself to heal.

THIS JOURNAL IS YOUR SAFE SPACE

Refrain from passing judgment on yourself, and avoid criticizing the choices you've made in your life. Instead, think of them with empathy and compassion. Consider what you learned from the experience and how it influenced you. The more you let go, the easier it will be to discover what's buried deep inside your subconscious mind.

When you revisit what caused you pain, anxiety can arise. It's important to remember that when your body is used to dealing with trauma, it's normal to feel abnormal. Grief, rage, doubt, and other negative emotions became familiar to your body. It's strange for your body and mind to let go and recover from traumatic experiences that you've been unconsciously holding on to for so long.

If you're feeling overwhelmed, take frequent breaks and go slowly.

TEND TO YOUR WOUNDS WITH CARE, AND LET YOUR EMOTIONS COME THROUGH WITHOUT FEAR

Consider your life as a series of chapters, each of which will reveal a layer of yourself to yourself. Draw stuff, add images, and don't be afraid to be creative when telling your story; believe in yourself. Recall your first memory using all five of your senses, and describe your emotions with as much detail. Recognize your progress as you catch up to your current self, because we often forget how far we've come.

...

THERE IS NO AGONY
LIKE BEARING AN UNTOLD
STORY INSIDE YOU.
—ZORA NEALE HURSTON

IT ALL BEGINS WITH YOU.

EVEN THE FAINTEST
CHANGE CAN RESULT IN
SIGNIFICANT GROWTH.

EVENTUALLY WE OUTGROW OUR OLD SELVES TO EMBRACE THE NEW.

AND ONCE WE'VE IDENTIFIED WHO WE ARE, IT'S EASIER TO UNDERSTAND WHY WE'VE BECOME.

WE LEARN WHAT
WE NEED IN ORDER
TO GROW.

FROM THERE WE'RE ABLE
TO BLOOM AND MAKE ROOM FOR
NEW OPPORTUNITIES.

AND IT ALL BEGAN WITH YOU.